WITHDRAWN

# Animal 911
## ENVIRONMENTAL THREATS

# Animals and Deforestation

## MATTESON CLAUS

Gareth Stevens
Publishing

Please visit our website, www.garethstevens.com
For a free color catalog of all our high-quality books,
call toll free 1-800-542-2595 or fax 1-877-542-2596.

Library of Congress Cataloging-in-Publication Data

Claus, Matteson.
Animals and deforestation / by Matteson Claus.
 p. cm. — (Animal 911: environmental threats)
Includes index.
ISBN 978-1-4339-9707-5 (pbk.)
ISBN 978-1-4339-9708-2 (6-pack)
ISBN 978-1-4339-9706-8 (library binding)
1. Deforestation—Juvenile literature. I. Claus, Matteson. II. Title.
SD418.C53 2014
634.95—dc23

First Edition

Published in 2014 by
**Gareth Stevens Publishing**
111 East 14th Street, Suite 349
New York, NY 10003

© 2014 Gareth Stevens Publishing

Produced by Planman Technologies
Designed by Sandy Kent
Edited by Jon Bogart

Photo credits: Cover : taolmor/123RF; Background : LeksusTuss/Shutterstock.com; Inside: Pg 4: Four Oaks/Shutterstock.com; Pg 5(l): Frontpage/Shutterstock.com; Pg 5(r): Robert Biedermann/Shutterstock.com; Pg 6: non15/Shutterstock.com; Pg 7(t): Ivan_Sabo/Shutterstock.com; Pg 7(b): danymages/Shutterstock.com; Pg 8: Ales Liska/Shutterstock.com; Pg 9: Fabien Monteil/Shutterstock.com; Pg 10: Photoshot/IndiaPicture; Pg 11: A_Sh/Shutterstock.com; Pg 12: NASA/Goddard Space Flight Center Scientific Visualization Studio; Pg 13: StephenE/Shutterstock.com; Pg 14(t): ©blickwinkel/Alamy/IndiaPicture; Pg 14(b): Hung Chung Chih/Shutterstock.com; Pg 15: ©blickwinkel/Alamy/IndiaPicture; Pg 16(t): Eye Ubiquitous/IndiaPicture; Pg 16(b): ©Zoonar GmbH/Alamy/IndiaPicture; Pg 17: Tony Campbell/Shutterstock.com; Pg 18: ©All Canada Photos/Alamy/IndiaPicture; Pg 19: Image Broker/IndiaPicture; Pg 20: ©Reinhard Dirscherl/Alamy/IndiaPicture; Pg 21: ©Roger Bamber/Alamy/IndiaPicture; Pg 22: Nick Biemans/Shutterstock.com; Pg 23: Photoshot/IndiaPicture; Pg 24: ©Victor St. John/Alamy/IndiaPicture; Pg 25: Ewan Chesser/Shutterstock.com; Pg 26: Murray Cooper/Minden Pictures/Getty Images; Pg 27: Murray Cooper/Minden Pictures/Getty Images; Pg 28: Aldo Brando/Stone/Getty Images; Pg 29: ©GM Photo Images/Alamy/IndiaPicture; Pg 30: ©Arco Images GmbH/Alamy/IndiaPicture; Pg 31: Elmer Martinez/AFP/Getty Images; Pg 32: Stephane Bidouze/Shutterstock.com; Pg 33: Sergey Uryadnikov/Shutterstock.com; Pg 34: ©National Geographic Image Collection/Alamy /IndiaPicture; Pg 35: stephen/Shutterstock.com; Pg 36: Photoshot/IndiaPicture; Pg 37: ©Jim West/Alamy/IndiaPicture; Pg 38: Anankkml/Dreamstime; Pg 39: ©Neil McAllister/Alamy/IndiaPicture; Pg 40(t): Nikonia/Dreamstime; Pg 40(b): joyfull/Shutterstock.com; Pg 41: Justin Black/Shutterstock.com; Pg 42: ©Humberto Olarte Cupas/Alamy/IndiaPicture; Pg 43: ©david tipling/Alamy/IndiaPicture; Pg 44: ©John Cancalosi/Alamy/IndiaPicture; Pg 45: Dtfoxfoto/Dreamstime.

t=Top, b= Bottom, l=Left, r=Right.

Printed in the United States of America

CPSIA compliance information: Batch #CS13GS. For further information contact Gareth Stevens, New York,
New York at 1-800-542-2595.

# Contents

Words in the glossary appear in **bold** type the first time they are used in the text.

# What Happened to the Forest?

It's a cool fall day in 1986. A spotted owl leaves its home at the top of an old tree. It flies off to hunt for food. However, there is something seriously wrong with the **forest**, and the owl senses it. It's the trees. Many of them are gone. The owl swoops down to hunt among the few trees that remain to look for food, but all the open space has scared away its prey. The owl hoots to find a mate, but its mate has been frightened and moved away. The spotted owl is hungry and alone.

A spotted owl searches for food.

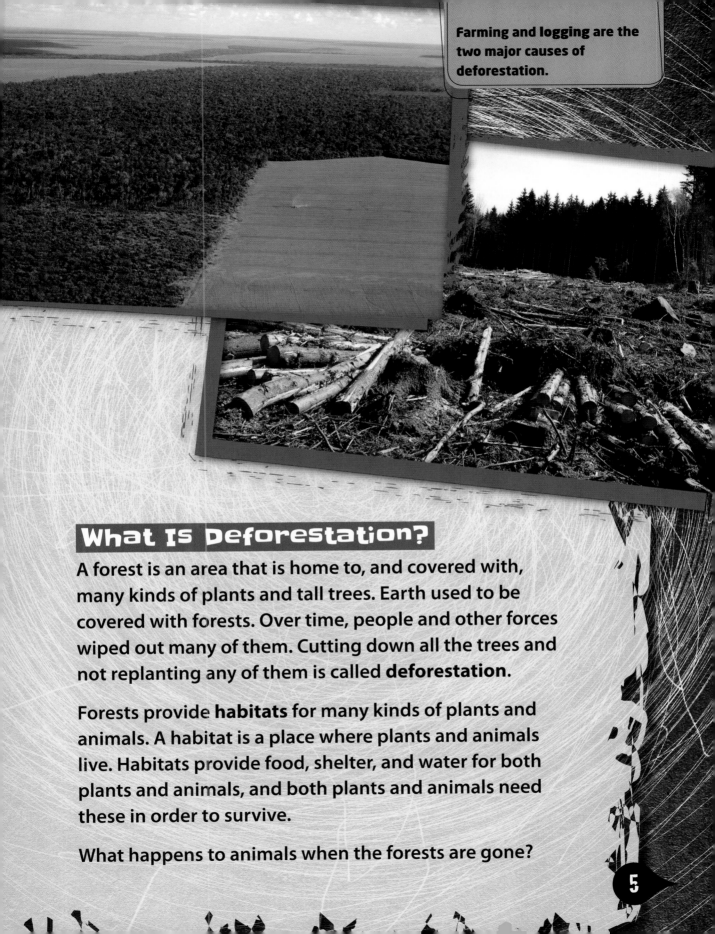

Farming and logging are the two major causes of deforestation.

# What Is Deforestation?

A forest is an area that is home to, and covered with, many kinds of plants and tall trees. Earth used to be covered with forests. Over time, people and other forces wiped out many of them. Cutting down all the trees and not replanting any of them is called **deforestation**.

Forests provide **habitats** for many kinds of plants and animals. A habitat is a place where plants and animals live. Habitats provide food, shelter, and water for both plants and animals, and both plants and animals need these in order to survive.

What happens to animals when the forests are gone?

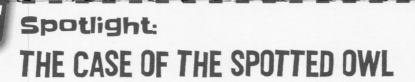

## Spotlight:

# THE CASE OF THE SPOTTED OWL

To understand how deforestation affects animals, let's take a look at the northern spotted owl.

These owls live only in **old growth forests** in the Pacific Northwest of North America. Since these forests are old, the trees are tall with open space on the ground underneath their branches. This allows the owls to fly under and between the trees. Old forests also have lots of good nesting places in the trees. These dense forests also provide lots of food for the owls.

In 1986, people began to realize that the spotted owls were disappearing. At the same time, their homes, the old growth forests, were being cut down. Was deforestation hurting the spotted owls?

Logging in the Pacific Northwest has severely damaged the habitat of the spotted owl.

# Causes of Deforestation

Why do people cut down trees and destroy forests? There are several reasons.

## Agriculture

One of the major reasons that people cut down trees is to increase the amount of land that is available for **agriculture**. As the need for food grows, farmers need more space to plant their crops. They also need **grazing** land for their **livestock**. People cut down forests to create the farmland they need.

Sometimes soil gets overused from too much planting. Sometimes livestock graze too much in the same place, which harms the soil, making it useless for grazing or for growing crops. To increase the amount of fertile land available for farming, more trees are cut and more forests are cleared. This cycle leads to deforestation.

Logging is a main cause of deforestation.

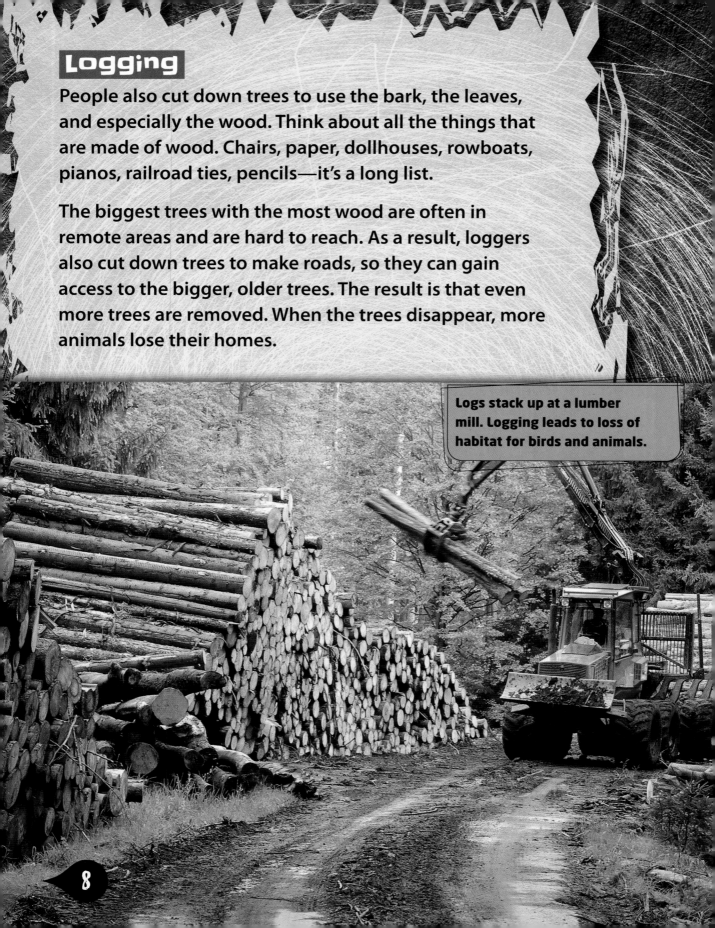

# Logging

People also cut down trees to use the bark, the leaves, and especially the wood. Think about all the things that are made of wood. Chairs, paper, dollhouses, rowboats, pianos, railroad ties, pencils—it's a long list.

The biggest trees with the most wood are often in remote areas and are hard to reach. As a result, loggers also cut down trees to make roads, so they can gain access to the bigger, older trees. The result is that even more trees are removed. When the trees disappear, more animals lose their homes.

Logs stack up at a lumber mill. Logging leads to loss of habitat for birds and animals.

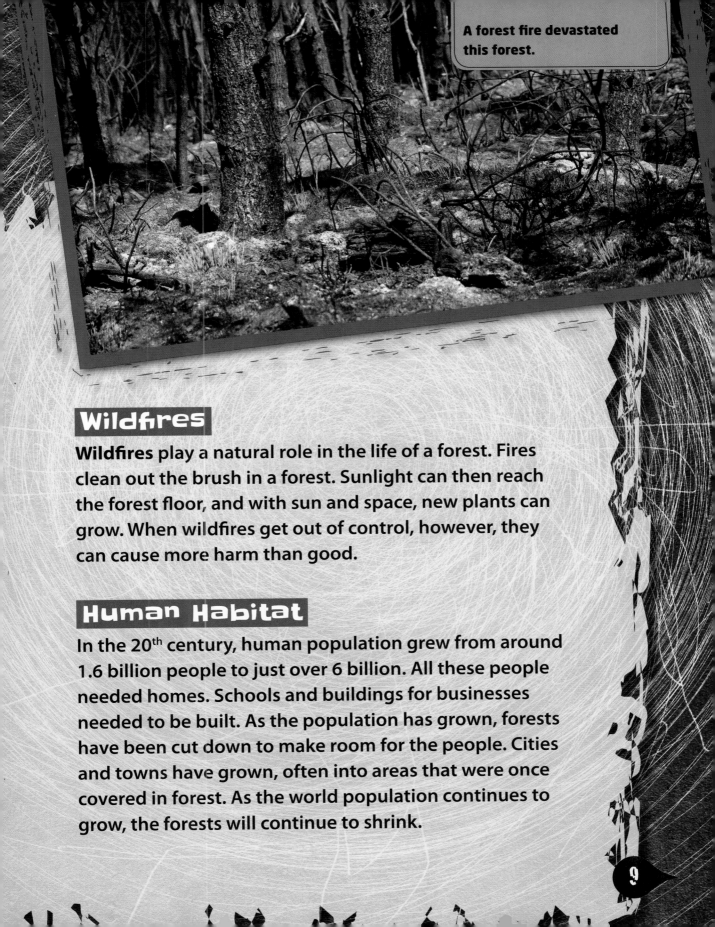

A forest fire devastated this forest.

## Wildfires

**Wildfires** play a natural role in the life of a forest. Fires clean out the brush in a forest. Sunlight can then reach the forest floor, and with sun and space, new plants can grow. When wildfires get out of control, however, they can cause more harm than good.

## Human Habitat

In the 20th century, human population grew from around 1.6 billion people to just over 6 billion. All these people needed homes. Schools and buildings for businesses needed to be built. As the population has grown, forests have been cut down to make room for the people. Cities and towns have grown, often into areas that were once covered in forest. As the world population continues to grow, the forests will continue to shrink.

# THE SPOTTED OWLS' MISSING HABITAT

People suspected that deforestation was affecting spotted owls. Why were the owls' home forests being cut down?

In this case, there were two main reasons. Some forests were cleared to make room for people to live. But mostly, people were logging the forests for wood.

The tall trees in old growth forests are an abundant, rich supply of wood. Wood is a valuable resource, used in many businesses and industries around the world. Logging also provided jobs to many people. These people depended on their jobs in the logging industry to feed and house them and their families. Logging was important to the economy, both locally and nationally. But what did the deforestation mean to the owls and their habitat? Where would they find homes, raise their young, and find food?

Workers cut down a tree in the Pacific Northwest. Logging is a major cause of deforestation all over the world.

# Effects of Deforestation on Animals

Deforestation has long-term harmful effects on humans, animals, and plant life.

## Loss of Habitat

Deforestation causes loss of habitat. When a forest is cut down, the animals that normally live there no longer have homes or food. Often if some of the original habitat remains, it is split up by roads, towns, and other barriers that animals cannot cross. Many animals need big areas to live in. They need plenty of food and room to hunt. When their original homelands are divided into smaller parts, animals lose their ability to forage and move freely in their natural habitats.

In addition, when a forest habitat is split up, animals get separated. Animals need to meet, roam together, hunt together, and mate. If they cannot do this, their lives are in danger.

## Climate Change

Deforestation changes the **climate** in several ways.

First, it affects the water cycle. When trees are cut down, they no longer evaporate water into the air. They no longer provide shade from the sun for plants and animals. Plants wither and die, and the soil dries out. The climate in the area becomes much drier.

With fewer trees and less water, the temperature changes. Many plants and animals cannot survive in the new, warmer temperatures.

As plants wither and animals die from these changes, there is less food for those that remain. With less food and water, even more animals will die.

This aerial view shows the effects of deforestation—bare, dry soil is all that remains.

# Spotlight:
# THE SPOTTED OWLS' DIRE SITUATION

Once the trees in the Pacific Northwest's old growth forests were chopped down, spotted owls had no place to live. The animals that the owls ate no longer had a home, either. They died or left. With no food and no home, the spotted owls began to die, too.

People soon realized that the owls' situation told them a lot about what was happening in the forest. The owls were a good example of how deforestation affected all the things that used to call the forest home.

As we will see later, people stepped in to help.

Spotted owls like this one are making a slow comeback in the forests of the Pacific Northwest.

13

Deforestation hurts pandas because they rely on bamboo as their main source of food.

# Bears

There are eight **species** of bears found in the world. Two types of bears in particular have been affected by deforestation.

## Giant Panda Bears

Giant pandas are black and white bears that live in Asia. They can grow to be about 5 feet (1.5 m) tall and weigh around 220 to 330 pounds (100 to 150 kg). The males are usually about 10 percent larger than the females. Giant pandas can live up to 20 years in the wild. In captivity, they can live up to 30 years.

A young panda cub is fed at a zoo.

In the wild, giant pandas live in forests that contain a lot of bamboo. Like other bears, pandas will sometimes eat meat, but bamboo is their favorite food. In fact, 99 percent of their diet is bamboo. Pandas can eat up to 84 pounds (38 kg) of bamboo a day! The bamboo forests also provide panda bears with shelter.

However, many of the pandas' home forests have been destroyed. Asia has a huge population of people, and the population is growing. To make room for the people to live and to grow more food, the forests have been cut down. Deforestation has left the pandas with far less food and shelter. In fact, there are only a few areas of forests left where pandas live.

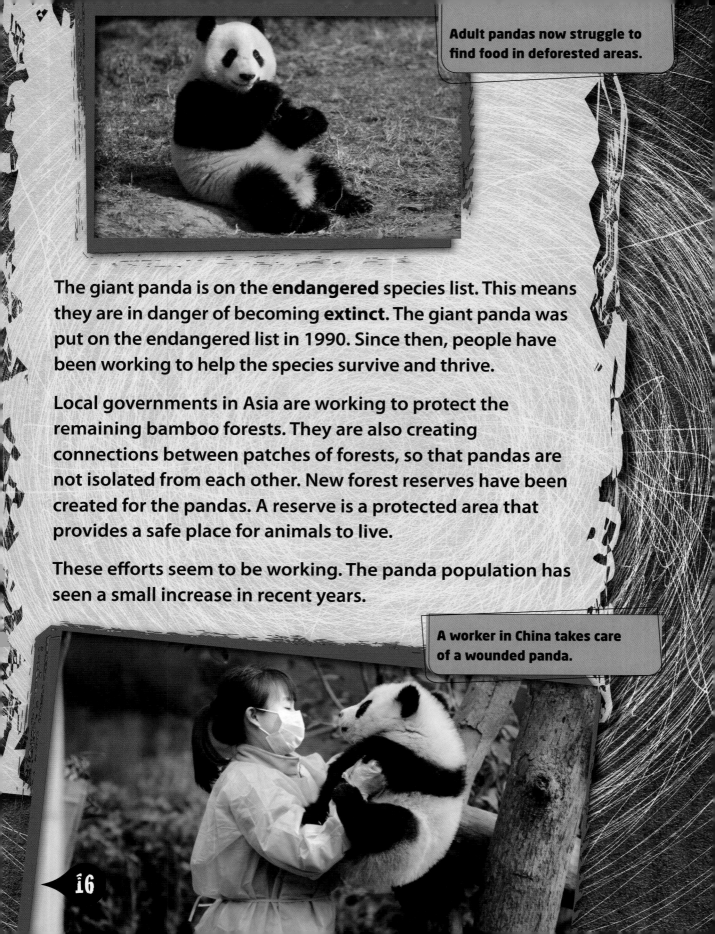

Adult pandas now struggle to find food in deforested areas.

The giant panda is on the **endangered** species list. This means they are in danger of becoming **extinct**. The giant panda was put on the endangered list in 1990. Since then, people have been working to help the species survive and thrive.

Local governments in Asia are working to protect the remaining bamboo forests. They are also creating connections between patches of forests, so that pandas are not isolated from each other. New forest reserves have been created for the pandas. A reserve is a protected area that provides a safe place for animals to live.

These efforts seem to be working. The panda population has seen a small increase in recent years.

A worker in China takes care of a wounded panda.

## Grizzly Bears

Grizzly bears get their name from the way their fur looks. Grizzly bears have brown fur, but the guard hairs on their backs and shoulders have white tips. This makes them look "grizzled" or gray-haired.

Like the pandas, grizzlies are big bears. A grizzly bear can grow to be 6 to 7 feet (1.8 to 2.1 m) tall. Most bears weigh between 300 and 600 pounds (135 and 270 kg). Sometimes, though, males can weigh over 1,000 pounds (450 kg). Although they are big, grizzly bears are fast. They can run as fast as 30 miles (48 km) per hour!

A mature grizzly bear hunts one of its favorite foods, salmon.

17

Human development impacts grizzly bear habitats. Here an adult grizzly bear crosses a road as it searches for food.

Unlike panda bears, grizzlies do not eat bamboo. Instead, they eat a variety of plants and animals, including fish.

Grizzly bears live in forests, meadows, and **tundra**. The bears once lived all across western North America. Now, they are only found in a few places. In 1800, there were approximately 50,000 grizzly bears in the lower 48 states of the United States. By 1975, there were less than 1,000. The grizzly bear is still the symbol on the California state flag. However, no grizzly bears have been found in California since the 1920s.

What happened? People cut down the grizzly bears' forests to build homes, to create roads, and to mine. Deforestation destroyed the grizzly bears' habitat, and when that happened, the bears were doomed.

With deforestation, the bears' habitats became isolated. They had less food and fewer safe places to live and raise their young. Grizzly bears eat a lot, and when their natural food supplies disappeared, the grizzly bears began to bother people, eating livestock, garbage, and even birdseed. Grizzly bears are ferocious, and they can be dangerous. As a result, people hunted the bears.

In 1975, grizzly bears were classified as a threatened species. Ever since, people have been trying to save them. Scientists have begun studying the bears by catching them and fitting them with GPS collars. GPS collars allow the bears to be tracked. Scientists are then able to use this information to create protected, linked habitats for the bears.

People are also learning how to live safely with the bears. Clever technology like electric fences and bear-proof garbage cans helps to keep the bears away from human populations.

As of 2011, grizzly bears were showing signs of recovery. People are continuing their efforts to help the grizzly bears survive.

This bear searches for food in a county garbage disposal site.

# Big Cats

Big cats include lions, tigers, leopards, and cougars. Most big cats have been affected by loss of habitat. To better understand the effects of deforestation on these cats, let's look at tigers and Amur leopards.

## Tigers

Tigers are the largest of the big cats. They are even bigger than lions! Tigers usually grow to be about 6 feet (1.8 m) long and can weigh up to 720 pounds (326 kg). Their fur is orange-red with dark stripes. Similar to people's fingerprints, no two tiger-stripe patterns are exactly alike.

Tigers like to hunt at night. Their striped coat helps them to hide and sneak up on their prey. Tigers eat meat, including snakes and crocodiles.

An adult Bengal tiger feeds on a kill.

20

Tigers live in the forests and swamps in Asia. Unlike other cats, tigers like water. They are good swimmers, and they never live far from water.

In the early 1900s, about 100,000 tigers lived in the wild. By the end of the century, three of the eight tiger species became extinct. Today, only about 3,000 to 4,500 of the giant cats remain in the wild.

Deforestation is a big part of the reason why so few tigers are left. People have cut down the trees, destroying entire forests, so they could use the wood from the forests for firewood and to make products like paper and furniture. They also cleared the land to grow food and crops like coffee, and to build homes.

As forests have disappeared, many of the animals that tigers depend upon for food have moved away or died off. The result is that tigers cannot find enough food. Like grizzly bears, hungry tigers prey upon livestock, an easy meal. This causes conflict with people, who then capture or kill the tigers to save their homes and animals.

There is hope. All species of tigers are now on the endangered species list, which helps to protect them. Several countries have set up protected living areas for the tigers. Further, some countries have also made it illegal to hunt tigers. Some groups are working to double the number of tigers living in the wild over the next 10 years.

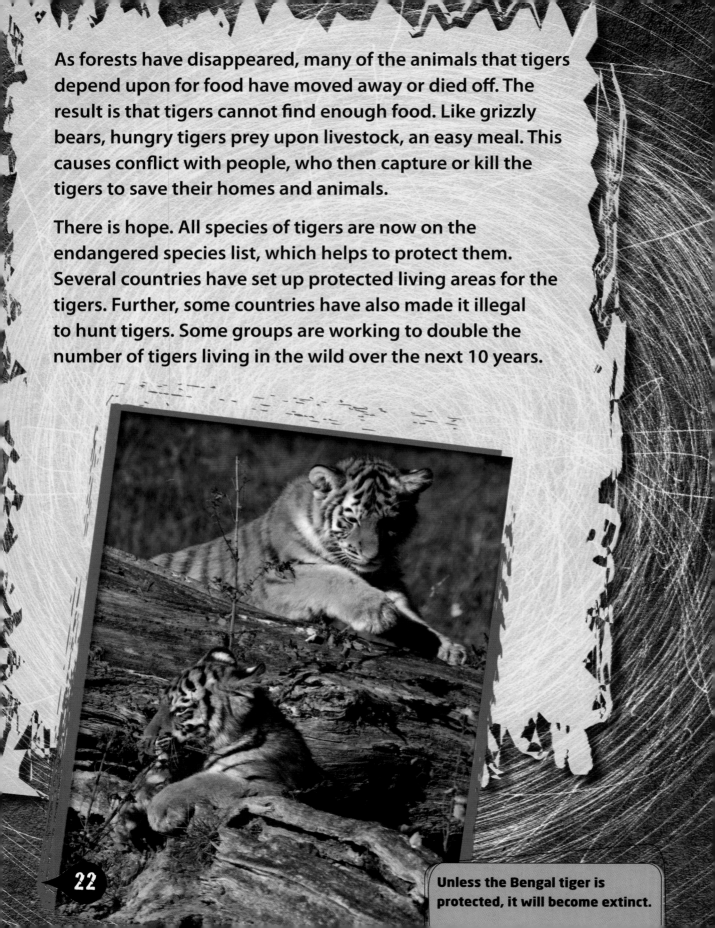

Unless the Bengal tiger is protected, it will become extinct.

An adult Amur leopard searches for food.

## Amur Leopards

Amur leopards are smaller than tigers. The males can weigh up to 120 pounds (54 kg) and the females up to 75 pounds (34 kg). Whereas tigers have stripes, Amur leopards have widely spaced spots with thick borders. Like other leopards, they can run fast—over 30 miles (48 km) per hour! They can also leap up to 10 feet (3 m) straight up and 20 feet (6 m) sideways!

Amur leopards live in northern forests in eastern Russia. These cats have adapted to their cold forest homes. In the winter, their reddish-yellow fur grows longer to keep them warm, and it also gets lighter so the cats blend in with the winter landscape. They also have longer legs than other leopards. This helps them to walk in the snow.

This pipeline project benefits people, but it is disruptive to the habitats of many animals.

By the mid-1980s, Amur leopards had lost about 80 percent of their habitat. People cut down the forests for wood and natural resources within the forest, to build roads and install gas pipelines, and so they could mine for minerals.

One of the biggest problems with deforestation in this region is that the leopards cannot find food or shelter. As trees are removed, people begin to farm the land next to the cleared forests, and eventually their farms take over land that was once forested. People hunt for food on the land that once held trees. Since people eat the same prey as the leopards, the leopards cannot find enough game to eat. They go hungry and starve.

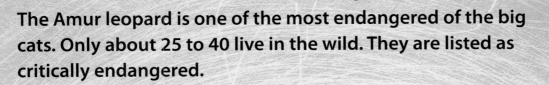

The Amur leopard is one of the most endangered of the big cats. Only about 25 to 40 live in the wild. They are listed as critically endangered.

In 2012, the Russian government created Land of the Leopard National Park. This park protects about 60 percent of the Amur leopards' remaining habitat. The government also decided not to build an oil pipeline through the leopards' forests. This decision is helping to save the leopards' remaining habitat.

It is hoped that now that Amur leopards have a safe place to live, their numbers will increase, and they will be saved from extinction. In addition, people continue to look for more ways to help save this beautiful big cat.

An Amur leopard blends in with the forest. Deforestation takes away its ability to hide easily.

# Birds

Many types of birds are affected by deforestation. Since birds live in trees, it makes sense that deforestation would have a particularly big effect on them. To understand this effect, let's look at two different birds.

## Yellow-Eared Parrot

Yellow-eared parrots are named for their yellow ear patches. They also have bright green feathers and dark beaks. These birds are about 17 inches (43 cm) high and weigh about 10 ounces (283 g).

These parrots are very social. They like to live together in colonies. Often, pairs will sleep side by side. They also travel together in flocks.

A yellow-eared parrot sits on a branch in the forest in the Andes Mountains.

The yellow-eared parrot population has been hit hard by deforestation. The birds live in only one area of the world—the cloud forests in the Andes Mountains in Colombia. Moreover, they live in only one type of tree in these forests. The yellow-eared parrots live, eat, and sleep in wax palm trees. As those trees disappeared, the numbers of birds dropped. For a while, they became critically endangered.

Wax palm trees are harvested for their leaves, which are used in religious ceremonies. When a tree is cut down, it takes a long time for a new tree to grow back. Then, to make matters worse, cattle often damage the young trees. The trees die before they are big enough for the birds.

Fortunately, people are helping yellow-eared parrots. Some people came together and purchased a part of the parrots' habitat. Then, they made it a protected reserve, giving the birds a safe place to live. As a result, in 2009, the number of parrots increased from around 80 to approximately 1,000. This increase in their numbers is very hopeful. The birds are still endangered, but they are no longer critically endangered.

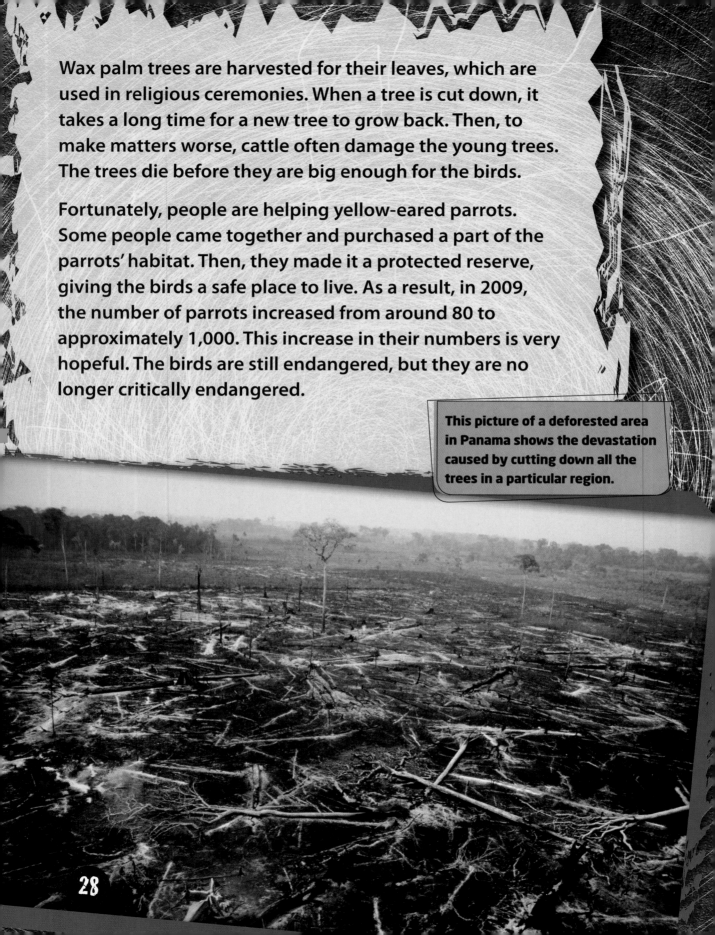

This picture of a deforested area in Panama shows the devastation caused by cutting down all the trees in a particular region.

## Harpy Eagle

Harpy eagles are named after the harpies in Greek mythology. Harpies were fierce creatures with wings, sharp claws, a woman's face, and a bird's body. One look at the harpy eagle's **talons** can help you see why they got their name. Their talons are as big as a grizzly bear's claws!

Harpy eagles are one of the biggest eagles in the world. They can weigh up to 20 pounds (9 kg), and their wingspan is about 7 feet (2 m) wide. Harpies are also one of the most powerful birds in the world. They can even catch big prey such as monkeys, sloths, and even small deer. They have great vision and fly super fast—up to 50 miles (80 km) per hour!

Harpy eagles live in the rainforests in South and Central America. Harpies build their nests in the tall trees of the rainforest. Many of their nesting sites have been destroyed due to logging, development, and agriculture. As a result, harpies are not having as many babies. Even when they do manage to find a place for a nest, they only raise one chick at a time. Then it takes a year to raise each chick. This means the number of harpies increases very slowly, if at all.

A harpy eagle chick waits for its mother in its nest.

A trained harpy eagle performs for an audience at a nature park.

Harpy eagles have almost disappeared from Central America. But, unlike the yellow-eared parrots, the harpies are not endangered yet. However, people are worried about how few are left. So, they are taking action to help save the harpies before it is too late.

Recently, Panama named the harpy eagle as its national bird. This helps to protect the bird. Also, some groups are working with Panama's government on **conservation** efforts. To help the harpies, people have begun studying the birds. Scientists and others who work in conservation are tracking the birds to learn about them and their habitats. The more that people learn, the better they will be able to protect the harpies and their homes.

# Great Apes

Great apes include bonobos, chimpanzees, gorillas, and orangutans. All of the great apes have been affected by deforestation. To get a better view of the situation, let's look at orangutans and chimpanzees.

## Orangutans

Orangutans are the biggest tree-climbing mammals in the world. Females weigh around 100 pounds (45 kg), while males can weigh twice that. Orangutans have very long arms. Some males have an armspan that measures 7 feet (2 m)! But they have short legs and are only about 5 feet (1.5 m) tall. When they stand, their hands almost touch the ground. Their long, shaggy fur is an orangey, reddish brown color.

Orangutans are big and strong, but they are no match for deforestation.

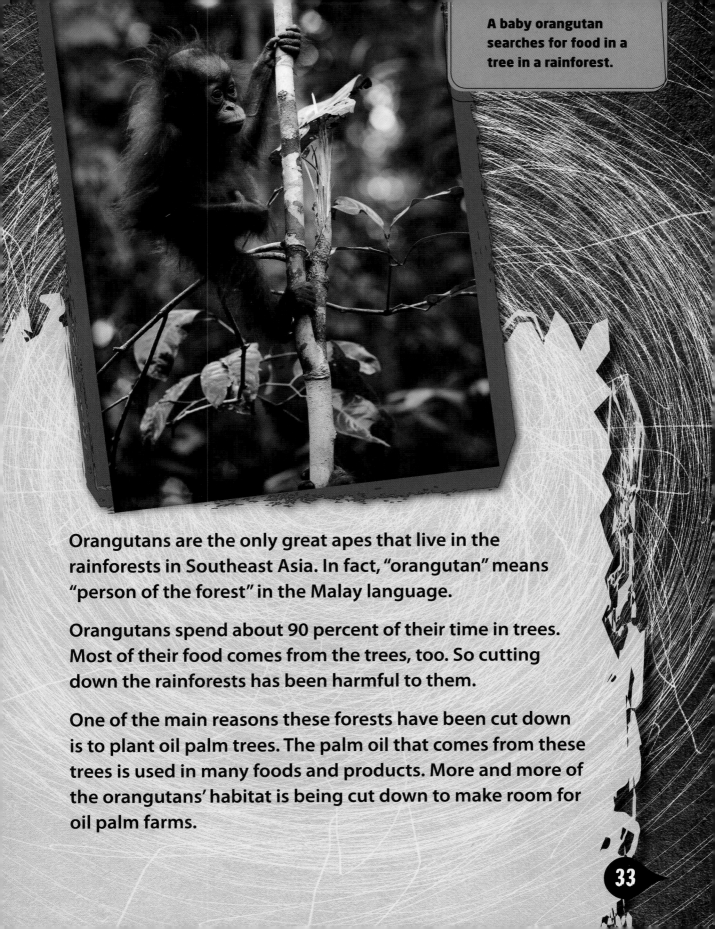

A baby orangutan searches for food in a tree in a rainforest.

Orangutans are the only great apes that live in the rainforests in Southeast Asia. In fact, "orangutan" means "person of the forest" in the Malay language.

Orangutans spend about 90 percent of their time in trees. Most of their food comes from the trees, too. So cutting down the rainforests has been harmful to them.

One of the main reasons these forests have been cut down is to plant oil palm trees. The palm oil that comes from these trees is used in many foods and products. More and more of the orangutans' habitat is being cut down to make room for oil palm farms.

With so much of their habitat lost, orangutans are now critically endangered. What are people doing to help them?

First, people are working to protect some of the orangutans' remaining habitat. They are also helping to link these areas. That way the orangutans can live and mate safely.

People are also working to improve the way that oil palm farms work. If farm techniques are improved and farms become more efficient, farmers will not need to cut down more of the rainforest to build new farms.

As these changes are made, hopefully the orangutans will be saved.

An adult orangutan eats grass and twigs in an open field.

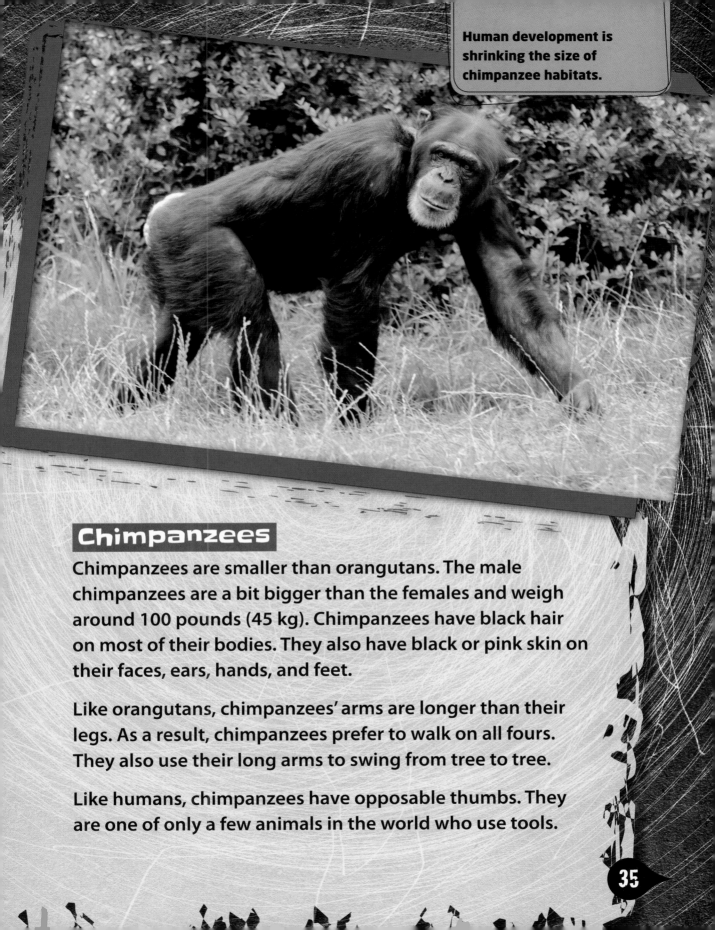

Human development is shrinking the size of chimpanzee habitats.

## Chimpanzees

Chimpanzees are smaller than orangutans. The male chimpanzees are a bit bigger than the females and weigh around 100 pounds (45 kg). Chimpanzees have black hair on most of their bodies. They also have black or pink skin on their faces, ears, hands, and feet.

Like orangutans, chimpanzees' arms are longer than their legs. As a result, chimpanzees prefer to walk on all fours. They also use their long arms to swing from tree to tree.

Like humans, chimpanzees have opposable thumbs. They are one of only a few animals in the world who use tools.

Chimpanzees live in Africa. They live in forests in countries near the equator. While they spend time on the ground, chimpanzees do most of their eating and sleeping in trees. Trees also provide them with food such as fruit, buds, and leaves. Chimpanzees also eat insects and mammals.

Over the past few decades, deforestation in central Africa has been severe. Now, there are only isolated patches of forests left. This has split up chimpanzee groups, so they cannot meet and mate. It has also meant a loss of food and homes.

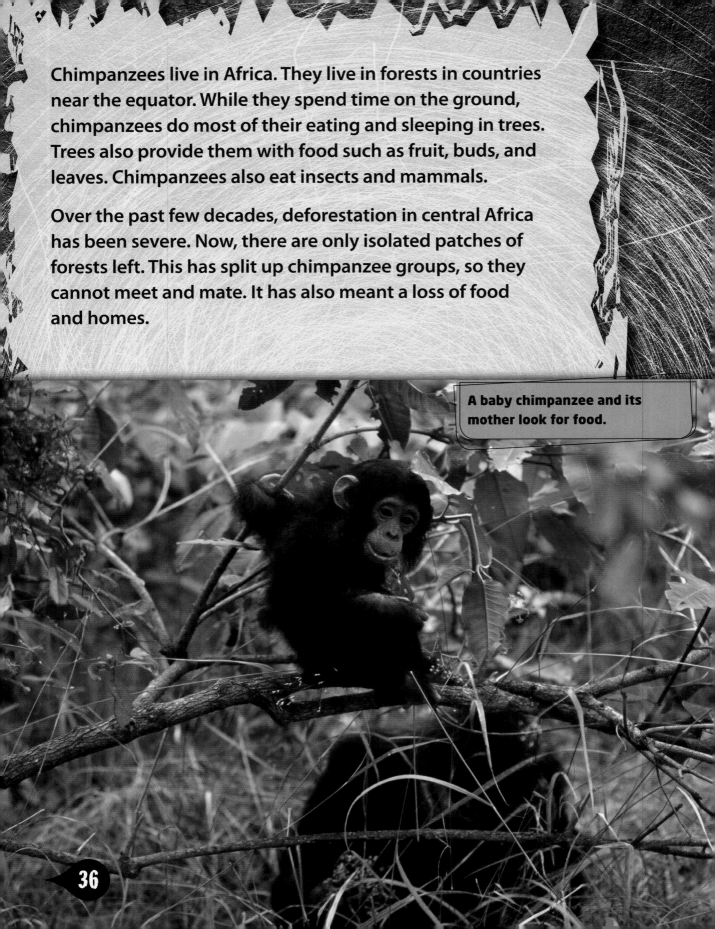

A baby chimpanzee and its mother look for food.

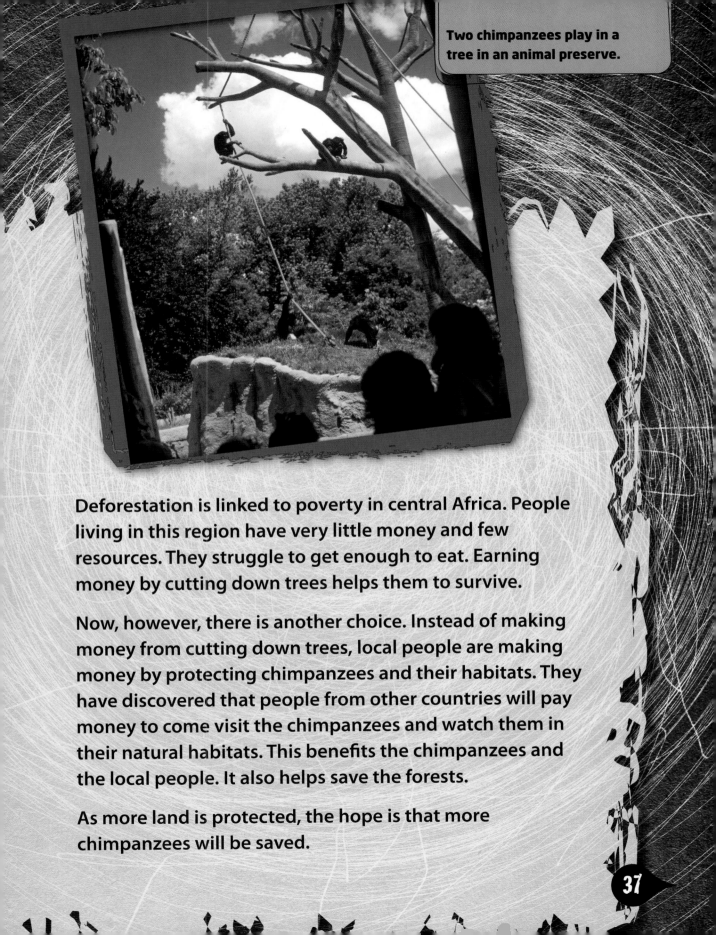

Two chimpanzees play in a tree in an animal preserve.

Deforestation is linked to poverty in central Africa. People living in this region have very little money and few resources. They struggle to get enough to eat. Earning money by cutting down trees helps them to survive.

Now, however, there is another choice. Instead of making money from cutting down trees, local people are making money by protecting chimpanzees and their habitats. They have discovered that people from other countries will pay money to come visit the chimpanzees and watch them in their natural habitats. This benefits the chimpanzees and the local people. It also helps save the forests.

As more land is protected, the hope is that more chimpanzees will be saved.

# Asian Elephants

There are two kinds of elephants: Asian and African. Asian elephants have smaller, rounder ears and overall they are smaller than their cousins, African elephants. Still, Asian elephants are big. They can grow to be 10 feet (3 m) tall and weigh as much as 11,000 pounds (5,000 kg)! The females are smaller than the males, though.

Asian elephants have long trunks. They use them like noses to smell and breathe. They use them like mouths to drink and to trumpet. Elephants also use their trunks like hands. The trunks have a fingerlike feature at the end that the elephants use to grab things.

A young adult Asian elephant walks through the forest. Deforestation is making it harder for Asian elephants to find food.

A big male elephant moves logs in a forest in Asia.

Asian elephants live in forests in south and Southeast Asia. The elephants eat plants, including leaves, bark, grasses, roots, and fruit. They eat a lot. An elephant can eat up to 300 pounds (136 kg) of food a day! As a result, they need a big habitat with lots of food.

The elephants have been losing their forest habitats. Like the other Asian animals, the elephants are competing with growing human populations. People cut down forests to make space for their homes and farms. They also build dams, roads, mines, and factories in what was once elephant habitat.

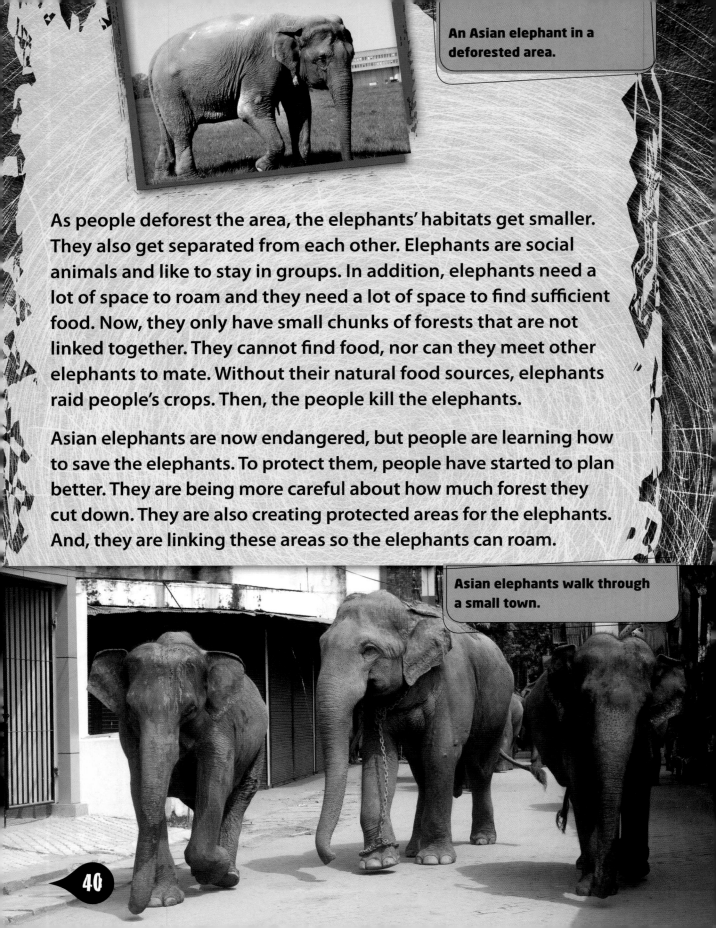

An Asian elephant in a deforested area.

As people deforest the area, the elephants' habitats get smaller. They also get separated from each other. Elephants are social animals and like to stay in groups. In addition, elephants need a lot of space to roam and they need a lot of space to find sufficient food. Now, they only have small chunks of forests that are not linked together. They cannot find food, nor can they meet other elephants to mate. Without their natural food sources, elephants raid people's crops. Then, the people kill the elephants.

Asian elephants are now endangered, but people are learning how to save the elephants. To protect them, people have started to plan better. They are being more careful about how much forest they cut down. They are also creating protected areas for the elephants. And, they are linking these areas so the elephants can roam.

Asian elephants walk through a small town.

# Golden Frogs

Mammals are not the only creatures affected by deforestation. Golden frogs are a good example of how deforestation can be harmful to **amphibians**. Amphibians are cold-blooded. When they are young, they live in water and breathe with gills. When they are older, they live on land and breathe with lungs.

Golden frogs are named for their skin color. It is bright golden yellow with black patches. The bright color is a warning to other creatures. These frogs are poisonous! These frogs may be small, but they are deadly. The females are bigger than the males. They can grow to be 3 inches (8 cm) in length and weigh 0.5 ounce (14 g).

Golden frogs are Panama's national animal. They live in the forests of Panama near running streams, where they mainly eat insects. These frogs have no eardrums. To talk to each other and attract mates, they wave their arms and legs. It's sort of like frog sign language!

Like the harpy eagles and the yellow-eared parrots, golden frogs have lost much of their habitat due to deforestation. People have logged the forests for wood and to make room to farm.

With its habitat disappearing, the golden frog became critically endangered. Then, things got worse.

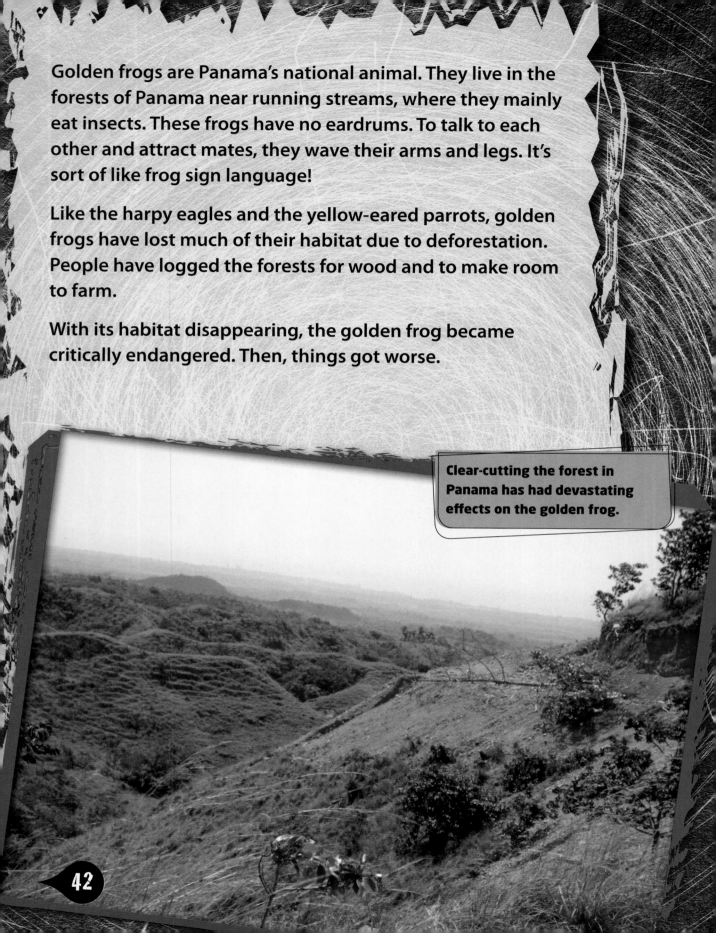

Clear-cutting the forest in Panama has had devastating effects on the golden frog.

The chytrid fungus has almost wiped out the golden frog. The fungus developed after part of the forest was clear-cut.

A fungus appeared in the remaining habitat. Some scientists think that the climate change caused by the deforestation caused the fungus. It is harmful to many kinds of amphibians. This fungus has killed nearly all the remaining golden frogs. They are about to go extinct in the wild.

To save golden frogs from extinction, some zoos have learned how to **breed** them in captivity. The frogs may still go extinct in the wild, but they will not be totally gone. Scientists hope to continue to breed them and increase their numbers. Thus, they are saving the golden frog from totally disappearing.

# Snot Otters

Another amphibian affected by deforestation is the snot otter. People have built roads and cut down forests near streams where snot otters live. The resulting pollution ruined streams and covered the places where the snot otters nested. Pollution destroyed the snot otters' homes, and it killed their food.

Snot otters are now considered threatened or endangered in many states. There is even more bad news for this species. The same fungus that is killing the golden frogs is killing the snot otters.

A snot otter lies motionless in a creek bed. Deforestation ruins creeks and rivers that run through forests.

# Help Is on the Way!

## Save The Forest, Save the Spotted Owl

To see how people's ideas are changing, let's look at what happened to the spotted owl.

People decided that it was important to save spotted owls. Saving the owl meant that some of the old growth forests had to be saved. In 1990, the US government named the spotted owl a "threatened" species. This meant that it was protected by special laws. Saving the spotted owls and their habitat meant that other creatures would be saved, too.

People will continue to cut down trees. But they can cut down trees without destroying a forest. Workers must consider how cutting trees in a forest affects all life connected to the forest.

CUTTING PROHIBITED

# Glossary

**agriculture:** cultivating land, and raising crops and livestock

**amphibians:** frogs, salamanders, and other cold-blooded vertebrates

**breed:** to reproduce by mating

**climate:** average weather conditions measured over a long period of time

**conservation:** preventing harm, loss, and waste of wildlife

**deforestation:** the result of converting forested areas to nonforested areas

**endangered:** in danger of dying out within 20 years

**extinct:** no longer existing

**forest:** an area covered with plants and trees

**graze:** to feed on grass

**habitat:** the surroundings where an animal or a plant naturally lives

**livestock:** animals raised for commercial purposes

**logging:** the process of cutting down trees and transporting them to sawmills

**old growth forests:** forests that have attained great age and great biodiversity

**species:** a single kind of living thing

**talons:** the claws of birds of prey

**tundra:** a treeless area between the ice cap and the forest line in the Arctic

**wildfires:** uncontrolled fires in the wilderness

# For More Information

## Books

George, Jane Craighead and Gary Allen. *One Day in the Tropical Rain Forest*. New York, NY: Harper Collins Publisher, 1990.

Napoli, Jo Donna and Kadir Nelson. *Mama Miti: Wangari Maathai and the Trees of Kenya*. New York, NY: Simon and Schuster, 2010.

## Websites

**International Union for Conservation of Nature**
*www.iucn.org*

The IUCN website acts as a clearinghouse for all things conservation, including information about deforestation.

**The Rainforest Alliance**
*www.rainforest-alliance.org*

The Rainforest Alliance provides information about forest conservation, biodiversity, and forest sustainability.

# Index